FROM CITY TO COUNTRY LIVING

FROM CITY TO COUNTRY LIVING

Arthur L. White and E. A. Sutherland

A Guide
to Those Making the Change

A Companion to the Booklet
Country Living

Review and Herald Publishing Association
Washington, DC 20039-0555
Hagerstown, MD 21740

Designer: Dennis Ferree
Cover Illustration: Dennis Ferree

Library of Congress Cataloging in Publication Data

White, Arthur L., 1907-
From city to country living.

1. Country life—Religious aspects—Seventh-day Adventists. 2. Seventh-day Adventists—Doctrines. 3. Cities and towns—Religious aspects—Seventh-day Adventists. 4. Urban-rural migration. I. Sutherland, E. A. II. Title.
BX6154.W457 1983 248.4'8673 83-13712
ISBN 0-8280-0222-3

PRINTED IN U.S.A.

Contents

Foreword

This booklet, first released in 1950, offers practical guidelines for those who want to enjoy life in a rural setting. It was published to accompany the pamphlet *Country Living,* which presented specific Spirit of Prophecy counsels. The E. G. White pamphlet has remained in print and has had a wide distribution, but *From City to Country Living* has been out of print for several years.

At the Annual Council of the General Conference Committee held in Takoma Park, Maryland, in October, 1978, church leaders voted: "That arrangements be made to republish the pamphlet *From City to Country Living,* so that church members contemplating a change in home location may have opportunity to secure and study this pamphlet, along with the counsel given in the pamphlet *Country Living,* by Ellen G. White."—*Adventist Review,* Nov. 23, 1978.*

The continuing demand for the booklet and the action of the Annual Council have led the publishers to make this helpful aid available once again. The reprint offers a few revisions, and several statements by Ellen White have been added. The book does not offer mere theory, such as a minister or administrator might expound. It is the earnest and practical advice of two men, both experienced in country living, who worked together under the auspices of the General Conference Commission on Rural Living.

"In the days before the Flood, every kind of amusement was invented to lead men and women to forgetfulness and sin. Today . . . Satan is working with intensity, that the same conditions of evil shall prevail. And the earth is becoming corrupt. Religious liberty will be little respected by professing Christians, for many of them have no understanding of spiritual things. . . .

* The full text of the comprehensive action calling the attention of the church to this vital matter is given as an appendix. See page 62.

"At such a time as this, the people who are seeking to keep the commandments of God should look for retired places away from the cities. Some must remain in the cities to give the last note of warning, but this will become more and more dangerous to do."—Manuscript 85, 1908.

The Story Back of This Booklet

Two men of divergent experience but knit together by a common interest, each with unbounded confidence in Ellen White's inspired messages, wrote this booklet. The older man, an educator and physician, often lovingly referred to Ellen White as "Mother," as did many others who knew her and worked by her side in her later years. The younger man could rightfully call her "Grandmother," but seldom did, for in his position he felt that he must relate to her as any Seventh-day Adventist would.

The older man was Dr. E. A. Sutherland. While serving as president of Battle Creek College in 1901, he listened to Ellen White's message to the General Conference session of that year. She urged the church to relocate Battle Creek College in a rural area where there would be ample land for cultivation. Boldly, and with faith in his heart, he and Percy T. Magan soon found an excellent site at Berrien Springs, Michigan. Within a few months' time the move was completed. School opened that fall, and classes met in tents and in the county courthouse.

Three years later Dr. Sutherland, Professor Magan, and Miss M. Bessie DeGraw founded Madison College—a self-supporting institution situated on a large farm near Nashville, Tennessee. Sutherland knew by experience what it meant for an educational institution to develop on a spread of several hundred acres, including rich river bottom as well as rolling pasture. He had personally participated in purchasing stock, milking cows, and peddling butter and eggs in the nearby city. He actively helped the students and faculty blend schoolwork with agricultural and mechanical pursuits. He knew what it was, with cash desperately short, to be responsible not only for hundreds of students but also for the many staff members and their families.

Sutherland had explicit faith in Ellen White's call for Adventists to choose a rural setting for their homes. He encouraged families to move into the great rural southland of America, where they could demonstrate practical farming methods. He appealed to them to set up little schools that would give the children in the communities an opportunity to gain an education. By being one with them, he knew their joys, their successes, and, in some cases, their failures.

The coauthor, Arthur White, was born and reared on a tract of wooded land adjoining Ellen White's Elmshaven estate in northern California. After purchasing the 59.5 acres of valley and hill land, Ellen White gave 7 acres to her son William and forbade him to sell any of it. She wanted it to be "the children's schoolroom and playground."

One acre and a half of cleared creek bottomland was especially well adapted to agriculture—orchard, berry patch, vineyard, and garden. Here young Arthur learned the rudiments of a number of basic skills, for if a carpenter or plumber was needed for some repair work, Arthur was often expected to "help" the craftsman, even if it meant skipping a day or two of school. During the gardening season, William White, when he was home, would require his children to work an hour with him in the garden before breakfast. Often on Sundays and evenings he would draw on them for assistance in splitting wood, building fences, cutting trees, repairing the road, et cetera. Arthur also learned animal husbandry, as milk was supplied by a Jersey cow, or Saanen or Toggenburg goats. A flock of White Leghorn chickens produced eggs for the White family.

Many times since those early years Arthur has commented that his grandmother's admonition that the seven acres provide "the children's schoolroom and playground" met a satisfactory fulfillment. It was not strange, then, that later when he and his wife, Frieda, moved from Madison College (where he served in the business office) to assist his father in the Elmshaven office, Arthur chose an orchard site for his own home. Here he continued to pursue agricultural and other practical activities as spare time allowed.

Understandably, when the work of the Ellen G. White Estate was moved to Washington, D.C., after the death of W. C. White, Arthur and his wife purchased three acres of wooded land in Maryland five miles from the General Conference office. Since this move occurred during the depression years, their start on the new place was modest and slow.

At that time chain saws were not common, so Arthur cleared the land with an ax and crosscut saw. Pick and shovel, at times augmented by a bulldozer, were used to dig out stumps and ready a portion of the land for a garden. Cows and chickens helped supply the food for their family, which now included three growing boys. At first the family carried water to the house from a nearby spring. Later, a rather poor well provided for baths, washing, and at times for a minimum of irrigation. Heat came from the trees cleared from the garden plots, and lumber to build a barn was milled from the oaks and pines Arthur felled and had sawed into lengths at a nearby mill.

When the Rototiller replaced the horse-drawn plow, it greatly simplified the gardening process. Each year Arthur would plow just a little deeper and would add manures and compost (and a little commercial fertilizer when needed). Quickly the virgin red clay soil improved, and soon the garden became very productive.

In 1950, when Dr. Sutherland helped write *From City to Country Living,* he also resided in Takoma Park, Maryland, and served as the secretary of the General Conference Commission on Rural Living. As he and Arthur prepared this practical guide, they drew from their own rich experiences in country living.

Three decades have now passed, and Dr. Sutherland rests from his busy and fruitful life. Arthur and Frieda White still own the little house five miles from the General Conference office. They continue to tend a garden, which provides them with outdoor exercise from spring through fall. Arthur's basement workshop gives him an opportunity for recreational activity in the winter. Although officially retired, Arthur spends most of the normal working hours in study and writing.

So after a lifetime of country living, Arthur, as the younger and surviving author of *From City to Country Living,* has made a few minor changes in the text—such as allowing for chain saws and Rototillers, which have made certain burdensome tasks so much simpler, and adding some pertinent quotations from his grandmother. He is glad to tell everyone that country living really does work!

The Publishers

The Call to Leave the Cities

Shortly after World War II ended there sounded with renewed emphasis among Seventh-day Adventists the call of God to leave the cities and locate their homes in rural areas. This call was brought with impressive force to the attention of Seventh-day Adventists throughout North America by articles in their church paper, the *Review and Herald* [now *Adventist Review*], and particularly by the publication of the pamphlet entitled *Country Living*. This pamphlet contained a compilation of the messages given by Ellen G. White from 1902 to 1906, and written by her in numerous manuscripts.

To many Adventists these statements were new. To others who had known of them their republication in 1946 was clothed with a new significance. A deep impression was at once created throughout the churches that this renewed call was timely and demanded study and action. A remarkable interest was taken in this call to leave the cities. Indeed, for a time some uneasiness was felt lest there should develop a mass movement and families might act on impulse without adequate and intelligent planning and businesslike arrangement, and thus bring disaster and disappointment to themselves and to the cause. This, we are glad to say, did not occur, and ought not to occur. If the instruction regarding procedure accompanying the heavenly messages is heeded, it will not occur.

The profound interest taken by Adventists generally may be discerned when the circulation of *Country Living* is considered. It was thought by the publishers that a printing of five thousand copies would be ample to supply the unknown demand.

Just before printing, this was increased to ten thousand copies, and that was the number of the first printing. This was completely exhausted within a few weeks, and a second printing of ten thousand copies became necessary. This was followed quickly by a third ten thousand; then by a fourth and a fifth printing, and through the years successive printings.

The effect has been gratifying and impressive. There has been serious study, followed by positive action. As families have found the way to do so, there has been a growing movement out of the cities to country locations. There have been careful plans, satisfactory and prudent arrangements, thorough inspection of new locations, close consultation with church and conference officers, and wisely executed management in the moves that have been made. Only in a very small number of instances has a hasty or indiscreet move resulted in consequences that have been regretted. This is the way the whole enterprise should continue to develop. And it is to help in this, and to answer as helpfully as possible the many questions to which any such movement gives rise, that this companion pamphlet to *Country Living* is published.

With Prayer and the Spirit's Guidance

As always in connection with developments of this sort there are those who misunderstand either the instruction given or their responsibility and duty with reference to it. There are also, unfortunately, those who seek personal gain in unloading undesirable real estate or profiting from the sale of land and buildings or developing colonizing projects. There are those as well whose business judgment has always been unsound and unsafe, who have failed in everything they have formerly undertaken, who are always eager to try something new and who attach themselves to any project in the hope that, at last, they will stumble onto success. These we shall ever have with us, and all we can do, as is done again and again in the instruction given in *Country Living,* is to sound urgent cautions, to appeal to good business sense, and to safeguard as far as possible against deliberate exploitation. We cannot emphasize too strongly or repeat too often the constant necessity that every move be made and every decision be taken in close counsel with church and conference authorities, with competent men and women, and with earnest prayer for the Spirit's guidance.

Seventh-day Adventists believe that the instruction and

counsel presented in *Country Living* has been given to them of God to warn and counsel and guide. They are sincere in their desire to avoid the hazards that they know are associated with city living, and to gain the blessings that accompany choice of a rural location for a home. To many families this will mean not only a change in the location of dwelling but also an adjustment in the employment by which family income is gained. These major changes involving residence and income are not only far-reaching in their influence; they are vital to the survival of the family. The questions now asked by many in our churches as they contemplate the call of God are: Where shall we live? What shall we do? How shall we make a beginning?

In *Country Living* a solemn caution is sounded against moving presumptuously. If there was ever a time for guarded, intelligent planning, now is such a time. Those who choose to change the location of their homes should have very definitely in mind just how they will gain a livelihood and what their employment will be. The Lord has not through the Spirit of Prophecy writings given detailed counsel as to how to meet all the problems that are certain to arise in making the major adjustments called for in moving from the city to the country. Nor is it possible for anyone or any committee to specify all the requirements or give counsel to cover every point. The circumstances of families differ; each family presents a distinct case. There are, however, certain general principles, which may well serve as a safeguard and a guide to those who are beginning to turn their eyes toward a rural environment for their homes.

The Decision Is Wholly Your Own

From the first step every move must be made intelligently and prayerfully. Too much is involved to take one step in the dark. Do not lean upon others, not even upon the church. Realize from the beginning that the decision you have to make is wholly your own, and you alone are responsible for making it. Get all the counsel you can, but make your own decisions. Your church cannot select a location for you. You must select it. Your church cannot make you a success in the work you decide to enter upon, or the enterprise you choose. Your church cannot make you a profitable farmer. Your church cannot till your ground, plant your crops, reap your harvests, sell your produce, or regulate your hours.

One man wrote, "You have made it plain what the church does not do; now tell me what it will do." The answer is that it will do what it is commissioned to do—teach the truth. It is the depository of the truth; its business is to preach the truth. This it is doing when it passes on the call of Heaven to leave the cities. The responsibility for heeding and acting on that call is yours. Do not expect the church to move you, to locate you, to finance you, to equip you, to make your decisions for you. It is not commissioned for that purpose and cannot engage in such a work.

So get all the information you can to move wisely. Seek it from sources that know. Take all the counsel you can get from those who are informed. But above all, seek to learn the will of God for you in every decision you are called to make. He has commissioned His Spirit to be your counselor and guide even in the smallest matters. Make no move unless and until you know you are following the mind of the Spirit. Then you will have the assurance that you are where God wants you, that you are doing what He designs for you to do, and that the outcome will be what He chooses for you.

What Is Country?

"Educate our people to get out of the cities into the country, where they can obtain a small piece of land, and make a home for themselves and their children."—*Country Living,* pp. 10, 11.

To some, country living invariably means nothing but isolation from civilization—a removal from all other human beings to some remote point entirely cut off from easy commerce and connection with the world. They think of the prophecies of world conditions in the very last days when we will be called upon to flee to the mountains for our safety. Perhaps it is this definition of *country* that has led some to feel they were unprepared to cope with the problems of country living that would arise from following what they understand to be the counsel of the Spirit of Prophecy. Country living, of course, *may* mean isolation if those concerned so choose, yet such an interpretation of the meaning of the word *country* as used in the Spirit of Prophecy calling for Seventh-day Adventists to enjoy the benefits of country living is unfounded and erroneous. Isolation is not called for in country living as urged in the Spirit of Prophecy. In many cases there is a direct appeal to Seventh-day Adventists to locate themselves so that they may stand as light bearers in the community. They are called upon to reside in or near villages and towns or to move to rural areas where they might herald the message by precept and example. Note the full intent of these words:

"Close around us are cities and towns in which no efforts are made to save souls."—*Christian Service,* p. 180.

"Missionaries are wanted to go into towns and villages and raise the standard of truth, that God may have His witnesses scattered all over the land, that the light of truth may penetrate where it has not yet reached, and the standard of truth be raised where it is not yet known."—*Testimonies,* vol. 2, p. 115.

To determine what may be considered as acceptable as a country location, we have several typical, concrete cases of comments upon the locations of certain well-known Seventh-day Adventist institutions. Observe the factors, desirable and undesirable, that are incidentally referred to.

In 1903, when a site was being sought for the factory of the Review and Herald, and the committee was searching in the vicinity of New York, we were counseled that "any place within thirty miles of that city would be too near."—*Review and Herald,* Aug. 11, 1903. The need of a sanitarium "in the vicinity of New York City" was urged upon us, and we were to search for locations "just out from the large cities, where suitable buildings may be secured" and used for institutional work and as a worker base (*Medical Ministry,* p. 308).

In southern California, Ellen White saw "the gracious leading of God" in preparing the way for us to begin the work of the Paradise Valley Sanitarium "a few miles [seven] south of San Diego" in bold contrast to the earlier intention of some who, seeming to have lost sight "of the plain instruction the Lord had given," "instead of planning to find some country location suitable for sanitarium work," "sought to establish a mammoth institution in the heart of the city" of Los Angeles (*Special Testimonies,* Series B, No. 14, pp. 3-5).

A Place "the Lord Selected"

In 1908 Ellen White recognized in Takoma Park, just on the edge of the District of Columbia and the City of Washington, D.C., a place "the Lord selected" for the establishment of "our printing house and our school and sanitarium" (letter 216, 1908). As soon as she and her helpers were comfortably located in Carroll House, where she was to make her home for a few months, she wrote:

"We are pleasantly situated at Takoma Park. Within fifteen minutes' walk are the homes of brethren Daniells, Prescott, Washburn, Spicer, Curtiss, Bristol, Rogers, Needham, Cady, and others connected with our work. . . .

"The location that has been secured for our school and sanitarium is all that could be desired. The land resembles representations that have been presented before me by the Lord. It is well adapted for the purpose for which it is to be used. There is on it ample room for a school and a sanitarium, without crowding either institution. The atmosphere is pure, and the water is pure. A beautiful stream runs right through our land from north to south. This stream is a treasure more valuable than gold or silver. The building sites are upon fine elevations, with excellent drainage.

"One day we took a long drive through various parts of Takoma Park. A large part of the township is a natural forest. The houses are not small, and crowded closely together, but roomy and comfortable. They are surrounded by thrifty, second-growth pines, oaks, maples, and other beautiful trees.

"The owners of these houses are mostly businessmen, many of them clerks in the government offices in Washington. They go to the city daily, returning in the evening to their quiet homes.

"A good location for the printing office has been chosen, within easy distance of the post office; and a site for a meeting house, also, has been found. It seems as if Takoma Park had been specially prepared for us, and that it has been waiting to be occupied by our institutions and their workers.

"My hopes for this place are high. The country for miles and miles around Washington is to be worked from here. I am so thankful that our work is to be established in this place."—Letter 153, 1904.

Within Easy Access of the City

We begin to see that whereas our institutions were not to be located in the cities, they were not in every case to be set up in isolated places. At the time the work was being started in Takoma Park, a group of workers was seeking a school site in middle Tennessee. Their plans to plant the institution at a point far from any metropolitan area were quickly altered as Ellen White, who was with them in this search, called attention to the advantage of being near Nashville. Here is her account:

"I was surprised when, in speaking of the work they wished to do in the South, they [Brethren Sutherland and Magan] spoke of establishing a school in some place a long way from Nashville. From the light given me, I knew that this would not be the right thing to do, and I told them so. The work that these brethren can do, because of the experience gained at Berrien Springs, is to be carried on within easy access of Nashville, for Nashville has not yet been worked as it should be. And it will be a great blessing to the workers in the school to be near enough to Nashville to be able to counsel with the workers there.

"In searching for a place for the school, the brethren found a farm of four hundred acres for sale, about nine miles from Nashville. The size of the farm, its situation, the distance that it is from Nashville, and the moderate sum for which it could be purchased, seemed to point it out as the very place for the school work. We advised that this place be purchased. I knew that all the land would ultimately be needed."—*Special Testimonies,* Series B, No. 11, p. 8.

Likewise, Mrs. White saw advantages to be gained in moving our New England Sanitarium from South Lancaster, forty miles from Boston, "to Melrose, a place much nearer Boston, and yet far enough removed from the busy city so that the patients may have the most favorable conditions for recovery of health. The transfer of the New England Sanitarium to a place so convenient to the city of Boston is in God's providence."—*Ibid.,* No. 13, p. 3.

When the congestion of Oakland, California, made it clear that we should move the Pacific Press to a less-crowded location, a site was found in the town of Mountain View, forty miles south of San Francisco and twelve miles north of San Jose. When Mrs. White inspected the situation, she wrote:

"One feels surprised that a place with so many advantages should not have been found before. This can be explained only by the false idea that our people have held that our institutions should be in the cities."—Letter 141, 1904.

In describing the place, she wrote:

"Mountain View is a town which has many advantages. It is surrounded by beautiful orchards. The climate is mild, and fruit and vegetables of all kinds can be grown. The town is not large, yet it has electric lights, mail carriers, and many other advantages usually seen only in cities."—*Ibid.*

And she was especially pleased because in Mountain View the workers could have homes surrounded by land that they could cultivate.

Note, too, Mrs. White's description of the proximity of Loma

Linda to certain small cities and of the particular advantage she saw in its location.

"'In the fall of 1903 I had a vision of a sanitarium in the midst of beautiful grounds, somewhere in southern California, and no property I had visited answered to the presentation given in this vision. . . .

"'While attending the General Conference of 1905, at Washington, D.C., I received a letter from Elder J. A. Burden, describing a property he had found four miles west of Redlands, five and one half miles southeast of San Bernardino, and eight miles northeast of Riverside. As I read his letter, I was impressed that this was one of the places I had seen in vision. . . .

"'Later, when I visited this property, I recognized it as one of the places I had seen nearly two years before in vision. . . .

"'One of the chief advantages of Loma Linda is the pleasing variety of charming scenery on every side. The extensive view of valley and mountain is magnificent. But more important than magnificent scenery and beautiful buildings and spacious grounds is the close proximity of this institution to a densely populated district, and the opportunity thus afforded of communicating to many, many people a knowledge of the third angel's message.'"—*Life Sketches,* pp. 405, 406.

It is plain that the satisfactory rural locations of these institutions brought them within convenient distance to centers of population and yet sufficiently isolated to gain the blessing of the country location. In nearly all these cases these institutions were within ten miles of a metropolitan area; yet in each case it was considered at the time of writing that they were located in the country. These approving counsels, describing the favorable country locations desirable for our institutions, provide guidance regarding what is meant by country living.

No Fixed Rule

Consideration must also be given to the fact that what would be country to one family may not be country to another. The family background, whether or not there are children, the ages of the children, the educational needs, the occupational skills, together with opportunities and special aptitudes for missionary work, are all factors that enter into determination of the case of each family as to just what constitutes country and the degree of isolation desirable.

Clearly Ellen White did not look upon country living as necessarily isolation from civilization. "Missionaries are wanted to go into towns and villages and raise the standard of truth, that God may have His witnesses scattered all over the land."—*Testimonies,* vol. 2, p. 115. The cities as well as the towns were to be benefited. "There will be laymen who will move into towns and cities and into apparently out-of-the-way places that they may let the light which God has given them shine forth to others."—*Review and Herald,* Sept. 29, 1891. The layman thus called to the city need not make his residence in the congested area. The cities are to be worked from country outposts. Another statement from *Testimonies,* volume 2, reads:

"Brethren who wish to change their location, who have the glory of God in view, and feel that individual responsibility rests upon them to do others good, to benefit and save souls for whom Christ withheld not His precious life, should move into towns and villages where there is but little or no light, and where they can be of real service, and bless others with their labor and experience."—Page 115.

Whether or not it would be wise for certain families to make their residence in or near certain towns or villages would depend on all the conditions that would have a bearing on the family and the opportunities to spread the message.

Whether residence is chosen in a village or town, in a sheltered place not far from a metropolitan area, in a purely rural area, or in the isolation of the wide-open spaces, we may apply the Spirit of Prophecy counsels, which would locate best the situation of our homes—"out of the cities," with their perils, "into the country, where" we "can obtain a small piece of land" (*Country Living,* p. 11). Where "the houses are not small, and crowded closely together."—Letter 153, 1904. In other words, where our light may shine to those in the country round about or to a nearby center of population.

Reasons for Moving to the Country

"There is not one family in a hundred who will be improved physically, mentally, or spiritually, by residing in the city."—*Country Living,* p. 13.

There are many reasons that may be set forth as arguments in favor of the family having its home in a rural location. These have been clearly and fully set forth in *Country Living,* but they are not recognized alone in the Spirit of Prophecy writings. Many educators and writers have sung the praises of the advantages of country living. We shall enumerate six major reasons here:

1. Best Environment for the Family

There is little need of arguing the point that a rural environment furnishes the most favorable conditions for rearing a family. It is greatly to the advantage of the children to grow up surrounded by the works of nature and by the activities of a rural home.

Even with the introduction of the television set into the rural home, the country atmosphere is more conducive to health and spirituality, and the routine chores, et cetera, are helpful users of leisure time.

No practical person would argue that the country home relieves the parents of all problems in the rearing of their children, but none will challenge the premise that the country home, with its interest and activities and its isolation from temptations of the city, greatly lessens the problems in rearing the family.

How much better it is for active boys to employ some of their spare time gardening, caring for the animals, cutting wood, repairing the fences, making furniture, doing the plumbing, and so forth, rather than for them to find their recreations on the street, at the neighbor's house with their friends, spending an inordinate amount of time viewing television, or perhaps at the theater or bowling alley. How much better for our growing girls to devote some of their spare time to the constructive activities of the rural home than to find time on their hands perhaps to be spent reading worthless books, watching the "tube," or attending some place of amusement. Then, too, the Christian will seek to locate himself in an environment that will contribute to, and not detract from, his making progress in his own personal Christian experience.

2. Opportunities to Spread the Message

We believe that we are in a world that is going down to its doom. We have a responsibility to make known to others that which is to take place and to help them to prepare for the coming of the Lord. All about us in rural communities are families who know nothing of our message. Again and again calls have been sounded through the Spirit of Prophecy for Seventh-day Adventists to enter such communities, make their homes in the villages and towns or in the country locations, and by their consistent lives and their missionary endeavors let their light shine. Note the Spirit of Prophecy counsel on this point:

"There are thousands who might enter the harvest field who are now religiously idle, and as a result, go crippling their way to heaven, expressing their doubt whether they are Christians. . . . I want to say to many, You are waiting for someone to carry you to the vineyard and set you to work, or to bring the vineyard to you, that you may experience no inconvenience in labor. *You will wait in vain*. . . . I think how the angels must feel seeing the end approaching, and those who claim to have a knowledge of God and Jesus Christ whom He hath sent, huddle together, colonize, and attend the meetings, and feel dissatisfied if there is not much preaching to benefit their souls and strengthen the church, while they are doing literally nothing. . . . If their temporal, financial prospects are not as prosperous by moving to localities where the truth has not been proclaimed, or where there has been but a glimmering of light, will they not be doing just the work that Jesus has done to save them?"—*Christian Service,* pp. 179, 180.

3. Cities Contain Elements of Self-destruction

Life in the large cities is becoming highly complex. The further people get from God's plan in their living, the more they become entangled. Part of the web constituting the elements that not only are detrimental but also lead to destruction is the fact that every individual in the city becomes dependent upon many other individuals. Any interruption in normal functions of service may lead to inconvenience and even to actual suffering.

Within these cities also the labor organizations have a much stronger position than in rural areas. At the slightest offense a strike may be called, which not only makes life uncomfortable, but at times imperils life itself. Not only do the strong labor factions exert their influence upon the consumer, but their activities may involve lines of employment in which we are engaged. This places a Christian in a very awkward position, recognizing as he does the principles of Christianity within the golden rule, and being coerced to join in activities contrary to the basic principles of Christianity. So the cities with their ever-enlarging problems, filled with vice and corruption, contain in themselves the elements of self-destruction.

4. Metropolitan Areas the Object of Enemy Attack

It is no secret that in times of war the metropolitan areas are the object of enemy attack. Knowing as we do that no peace plans will be permanent, we should give careful thought to the factor of choosing a safe location for our homes.

Though in times of peace it may sound well to assert that it is cowardly to think of running away from danger, yet the Christian, above everyone else, will be the first to plan for the security of his family. We would not think much of the parent who, in time of disaster, would leave his family uncared for, making little or no provision for their safety. Is the informed Christian, who knows from the sure word of prophecy that troublous times are coming and that there will be great distress in the cities, any less responsible in the matter of planning for the well-being and security of his family? We think the reader will agree that he is equally responsible.

The Lord Himself is interested in the comfort and safety, the well-being and security of His children. God in His love has presented to us a picture of the troublous times before us, and has repeatedly counseled us as to the proper provisions we should make to avoid suffering and perhaps loss of life itself in these troublous times. It is no indication of cowardice therefore to turn our backs upon the congested centers of population, and choose a rural location for our homes.

5. The Object of God's Wrath

Akin to the suffering that will come in the great centers of population in times of national emergency is the suffering resulting from the destruction in the great cities as God allows certain judgments to overtake them. Some have supposed that the destruction that falls as a judgment from God will come at the end of the world, but from the sure word of prophecy it is made clear to us that there will be great distress in centers of population as the wickedness of the cities reaches a certain point, and also as God through this means endeavors to arouse the inhabitants in these cities to the times in which we live and the need of making a preparation for the coming of the Lord. Note carefully these words recorded in 1906:

"I am bidden to declare the message that cities full of transgression and sinful in the extreme, will be destroyed by earthquakes, by fire, by flood. All the world will be warned that there is a God who will display His authority as God. His unseen agencies will cause destruction, devastation, and death. All the accumulated riches will be as nothingness. . . .

"Calamities will come—calamities most awful, most unexpected; and these destructions will follow one after another. If there will be a heeding of the warnings that God has given, and if churches will repent, returning to their allegiance, then other cities may be spared for a time. But if men who have been deceived continue in the same way in which they have been walking, disregarding the law of God and presenting falsehoods before the people, God allows them to suffer calamity, that their senses may be awakened. . . .

"The Lord will not suddenly cast off all transgressors or destroy entire nations; but He will punish cities and places where men have given themselves up to the possession of satanic agencies. Strictly will the cities of the nations be dealt with, and yet they will not be visited in the extreme of God's indignation, because some souls will yet break away from the delusions of the enemy, and will repent and be converted, while the mass will be treasuring up wrath against the day of wrath."—*Evangelism,* p. 27.

6. To Avoid Colonization

It is not God's purpose that Christians should gather in great centers to enjoy many advantages and remain idle. Whether these centers be the large metropolitan areas or the village in which is located a large denominational institution, there is the constant danger of colonization, and Seventh-day Adventists are called to scatter. The messenger of the Lord has written of this:

"Many of the members of our large churches are doing comparatively nothing. They might accomplish a good work if, instead of crowding together, they would scatter into places that have not yet been entered by the truth. Trees that are planted too thickly do not flourish. They are transplanted by the gardener, that they may have room to grow, and not become dwarfed and sickly. The same rule would work well for our large churches. Many of the members are dying spiritually for want of this very work. They are becoming sickly and inefficient. Transplanted, they would have room to grow strong and vigorous.

"It is not the purpose of God that His people should colonize, or settle together in large communities. The disciples of Christ are His representatives upon the earth, and God designs that they shall be scattered all over the country, in the towns, cities, and villages, as lights amidst the darkness of the world."—*Testimonies,* vol. 8, p. 244.

There are thousands who might remove to rural locations where they could continue their present employment in gaining a livelihood or take up new employment, and through the demands that would be made upon them, let their light shine in the darkened area and thus gain great benefits in their own spiritual experience. Other reasons might be mentioned why Seventh-day Adventists should choose a rural location for their homes. There are great blessings in store for families who select an environment for their homes among the objects of God's creation and as far as possible isolated from the many temptations and allurements in the cities.

God's Promises to Help Families to Locate Out of the Cities

"The time has come, when, as God opens the way, families should move out of the cities."—*Country Living,* p. 24.

There are many who would like to move to the country. But they ask, How can we do it? We have no large savings account; our family expenses consume about all our income; we know little of how to cultivate the soil. How can we move to the country? To such we would say that if it is the Lord's will that you should live in a rural location, at the proper time God will open the way. From the Spirit of Prophecy we have this admonition already noted above: "The time has come, when, as God opens the way, families should move out of the cities."

This is an issue we are not to force. All rash and careless moves are to be avoided. We must know where we are to go and what we are going to do for a livelihood when we get there. On the other hand, we are not to sit idly waiting for an opportunity to present itself. We are warned that "erelong there will be such strife and confusion in the cities, that those who wish to leave them will not be able. We must be preparing for these issues."—*Ibid.,* p. 11. It is said that "the Lord helps those who help themselves." We must show our faith and determination by taking the first steps.

The First Steps

Among the first steps are those that will prepare the family for country living. Before a move is made, study should be given to all that is involved. Read books and periodicals bearing on the subject. Make use of the public library. Hold meetings for discussion. Get a supply of the literature for free distribution or at a nominal cost from the United States Department of Agriculture, from your State Department of Agriculture, or from your county agent. One excellent brochure offers this wise counsel: "In farming, ten dollars' worth of borrowed brains will save you ten thousand dollars' worth of borrowed trouble."

Then pray about it. After placing the matter before the Lord, you may properly begin to look for a country home site. Let the search for the plan be a family project. Some families will buy a piece of land and will arrange to have a home erected; others will buy land with the buildings already on the property. Every step should be entered into carefully, intelligently, and prayerfully.

The Lord is deeply interested in all these matters that have to do with our welfare. He is the one who sounds the call for Seventh-day Adventists to seek country homes, and He is interested in our finding the kind of place that will suit our needs. So we work together, the Lord giving us counsel and instruction and caution, and through His providence opening the way, and we studying, preparing for country living, and seeking the type of place suited for our needs.

It is essential that we make a move in the right direction. How do we know what God may have in store for us if we do not begin to look around to see? There is much to be gained by getting the mind set toward the country. This will hasten the actual move to the new site. The family that waits for every question to be answered and every door to be opened will make no move. On the other hand, make no hasty move. Do not allow yourself to be stampeded into buying until you are sure you have found the right place. In all this experience there is much to be gained in waiting on the Lord.

Earnest Faith and Diligent Work

In our experience the Lord requires us to exercise faith, but great care should be taken to see that this faith is not presumption. It has been the experience of many who, under the conviction that they should choose a rural environment for their homes, have begun to take steps in the right direction that the Lord in a remarkable way has opened doors before them. We should not conclude by this that to make the move successfully most diligent labor and exertion are unnecessary.

We cannot sit down and fold our hands, and thus obtain those things the Lord would have us secure. While waiting and reading and keeping our eyes open for the right place, why not begin a garden? Some places, even in the city, have a little space for a garden; or arrangements can be made for use of a portion of a vacant lot. The experience gained in working the soil may save many a mistake when the work is begun in earnest in a larger way, and from the start it will prove a blessing.

Country living is not easy living, but neither our bodies, nor our minds, nor our souls are benefited by a life of ease or inactivity. Country living means activity. But with thorough planning this can be held to that amount of exercise that is beneficial. Those only who are first convinced in their hearts that it is God's will for their best good that they should move to the country and who are ready and willing to sacrifice and to labor diligently to make such a program a success can confidently expect success.

Although we have been told that families should move to the country *as the Lord opens the way,* we also have been informed that "many will have to labor earnestly to help open the way."—*Ibid.,* p. 25. Perhaps there must be some delay in taking the steps we would like to take. Be that as it may, let us make a beginning—a proper beginning.

A Time for Seeking Counsel

In this matter there is great need of counsel with those who have had practical experience in these things. With this we must mingle sound judgment and common sense. We must not let our enthusiasm blind us to the task ahead and to that which will be required to make a success of country living. Nor must we lose sight of trying situations that may come in life through following God's plan for His people in country home ownership. The chapter in *Country Living* entitled "Guided by God's Providences" should be read and reread by the family anticipating moving into the country. It is highly essential that no rash moves be made. None must in his endeavors and sincerity move presumptuously and then have occasion to regret the steps he has taken. There need be no great losses, with their resulting discouragement, if we seek counsel and move cautiously.

We close this chapter with two important paragraphs from the cautions found in *Country Living:*

"Let everyone take time to consider carefully; and not be like the man in the parable who began to build, and was not able to finish. Not a move should be made but that movement and all that it portends are carefully considered—everything weighed. . . . To every man was given his work according to his several ability. Then let him not move hesitatingly, but firmly, and yet humbly trusting in God.

"There may be individuals who will make a rush to do something, and enter into some business they know nothing about. This God does not require. Think candidly, prayerfully, studying the Word with all carefulness and prayerfulness, with mind and heart awake to hear the voice of God. . . . To understand the will of God is a great thing."—Page 26.

Choosing a Location for a Home in the Country

"The Lord desires His people to move into the country, where they can settle on the land, and raise their own fruit and vegetables, and where their children can be brought in direct contact with the works of God in nature."—*Country Living,* p. 30.

We now come to a very practical part of our subject. Having determined to leave the crowded metropolitan areas and make a home in the country, one raises the questions: Where shall I go? What kind of home shall I select? How shall we gain a livelihood? It has already been made clear that country living does not necessarily mean isolation from civilization. It should also be made clear that country living, if God's plans are fully followed, though it embodies some agricultural activities, does not mean that we must depend entirely upon the soil for a livelihood.

Country living is not a synonym for farming. Those who live in the country may choose farming as a means of livelihood, but a large number of people living in the country may, and do, gain a livelihood by other means.

That Ellen White so understood it is made clear by the wording of several of the statements made to encourage our people to country living.

"Educate our people to get out of the cities into the country, where they can obtain a small piece of land, and make a home for themselves and their children."

"Get out of the cities as soon as possible, and purchase a little piece of land, where you can have a garden."—*Ibid.,* pp. 11, 17.

It is vitally essential that the family planning to move to the country should keep in mind that there must be a definite means of income. The country-living family must be housed, must eat, must have clothes, must be kept warm, must be educated, must have means of transportation, just as the city family must have these things; and it takes money to supply these necessities and conveniences in the country, just as it does in the city. One point must therefore never be lost sight of, and that is *the family sustenance.*

Among the practical rules that must be established to guide our thinking in the choice of a location, we therefore place as of first importance family sustenance. Our decisions regarding this must be molded by choice between two objectives:

1. Gaining the benefits of a rural home, but looking to other means than the cultivation of the soil for sustenance.

2. Giving full time to agricultural pursuits and depending entirely upon the soil as a means of livelihood.

Only those who are fully prepared through proper training and background should attempt to farm for a living. To handle the soil so as to cause it to produce profitably and to conduct animal husbandry in such a way as to benefit financially call for intelligent operations and diligent labor. It can be done. Many thousands of families live bountifully and successfully on the farm. But no one should flee to the farm, burning his bridges of sustenance behind him, until he is sure by experience and training that he can successfully gain a livelihood year in and year out in that way of life. This is said not to discourage anyone, but rather to avoid the disappointment that comes to those inexperienced persons who feel that anyone can farm, and therefore, even though unprepared, turn to the soil for total sustenance.

The Rural Home for the City Worker

Now living in the cities are thousands of families who might enjoy the advantages of a rural home environment and still maintain their present employment. It is not uncommon for a city dweller to spend from twenty minutes up to an hour traveling from his residence to his place of work. With but a few exceptions such families could be living in a rural area, if rightly chosen, and the wage earner could travel to his place of work in about the same amount of time that is now required. In this way the family could have the benefits of the country location and the wage earner maintain his income status. The benefits justify even the extra expense incurred by extra travel.

With his children away from the sights and sounds of the densely populated area, and with a small garden in which may be gained the blessing of working with the soil and with the fruits of such labors to reduce the food budget for the family, the advantages of country living may be achieved without sacrificing the income of employment.

The Privately Owned Business

There are many today now employed in the city, perhaps working in some office or factory or in some trade, who could establish their own business in a rural location. The mechanic could set up his own shop and soon find nearby business furnishing a livelihood. The artisan could operate his own business, drawing largely from his neighborhood for his trade. The choice of the site for a home for such a family would take into account the business opportunities of a given location. Such a mechanic or artisan would want his business where it can be easily found, perhaps on some highway where the place of business itself would serve as advertising. There are scores of opportunities in these lines, and a little study of what others are doing and what can be done as it is set forth in easily available publications should be of service to the family seeking a rural home so situated that the wage earner could operate his own business. This small, self-operated business, shop, or factory is almost entirely free from government regulation and labor problems.

Depending on the Soil for a Livelihood

The wide-open spaces have their lure for some families. Fortunate are those who have been reared in the country and know from experience the joys and the satisfactions of farming, and are fully versed as well regarding the cares and responsibilities of such work. Should the family choose to operate a farm for a livelihood, the factors we enumerate for making country living a success should be taken into consideration. We must keep in mind our contact with the church and school and others of like faith, that our own hearts may be refreshed. We must ever keep in mind that our children must be reared in such a way as to benefit from the advantages of a Christian education and have the association of others of like faith, so that they may be able to choose as their companions for life those who will fellowship with them in their spiritual experience. This, perhaps, is more difficult for the family choosing the farm, but with proper study favorable situations may be created or found.

What to Watch for in Selecting a Home Location

In selecting the home location in the rural area the city worker or private businessman must keep several important factors in mind. It is difficult to know which are the most important. We present nine.

1. *Location in Relation to Work.*—The home should be located within relatively easy access to the place of labor of the wage earner. In these days of rapid transit, good highways, and family-owned cars such a location may be anywhere within a radius of five, ten, fifteen, or even twenty miles. Attention should be given to the matter of roads, their condition in winter, et cetera. It is well to be near or on a paved road or an all-year road leading to a highway. You are to be a light to the community. Do not hide in an inaccessible spot. Locate within reach of others.

2. *The Adaptability of the Property Should Be Considered.*—If possible, productive soil should be chosen. Such services as electricity and telephone should be available. In many rural areas city water and city sewers are not available, but these are not insurmountable difficulties. Attention should be given to the water level, making sure of a good water supply at a reasonable figure. A good supply of water is of first consideration. There should be trees, some pasture land and tillable land for garden, vineyard, and orchard.

3. *Proximity to School, Church, and Seventh-day Adventist Neighbors.*—Although Seventh-day Adventists are warned against colonization, the bringing together of large numbers of those of like faith in one place, it must ever be borne in mind that the success of country living for the family will be largely dependent upon the accessibility to a church and church school and Seventh-day Adventist neighbors. There should be public transportation to church and church school, or choice of location should be made in an area where there are several Adventist families that can form a small church, operate a church school,

and possibly a school bus.

The education of the children must be provided for, and the Seventh-day Adventist family that moves to the country will be satisfied with nothing less than a church school. Religious needs cannot be overlooked. Church attendance is essential. Nor can we pass by lightly the social needs. Seventh-day Adventists are not at ease or safe in seeking their social contacts solely with unbelievers. For the sake of the entire family, and especially our young people, the family should locate where there can be association with those of like faith.

4. *Home Ownership.*—It is desirable that the family should own its home. Note the implication of these words from the pen of inspiration: "Parents should *get as suitable a place as their means will allow.*" "Fathers and mothers who possess a piece of land and a comfortable home are kings and queens." "Get out of the cities as soon as possible, and *purchase a little piece of land,* where you can have a garden."—*Ibid.,* pp. 24, 18, 17.

Ellen White, in her own practice through the years, owned her own home. If the investment is made wisely, home ownership constitutes one of the soundest investments that can be made, and gives the family a security that can be had in no other way. In addition to the security of home ownership there comes a certain satisfaction and pleasure in the possession of a home property. The knowledge that any destruction of property willfully or through carelessness diminishes the family assets is also a worthwhile factor. This creates a sense of responsibility and carefulness that is not easily brought about when residence is in a property owned by others.

5. *A Clear Title.*—When purchasing, see that the land is unencumbered. Have the title searched by a competent person or firm. Money spent for such a service is good insurance. Have the deed recorded. Let there be no carelessness here. If unaccustomed to handling matters of this kind, seek reliable legal counsel.

6. *Family Garden.*—Careful attention should be given to the securing of a property where there can be a garden of both flowers and vegetables. Were there no financial returns from gardening, it would still be worthwhile from the standpoint of experience in tilling the soil and the lessons learned and the satisfactions obtained from working with growing things. But beyond this, if the

soil is worked intelligently, it will yield a harvest that will reduce the amount paid out for food. The nature of the soil, the time that can be devoted to the enterprise, and the skill with which the work is done are all factors in determining the returns.

Country living of this type has given birth to what one couple called "the have-more plan," for with the work of their hands the family can produce in their spare time at least a good portion of that which they would ordinarily have to buy or perhaps not even have at all. And don't forget: "A dollar saved is a dollar earned."

The family unskilled in agriculture should not expect to find their land yielding all that is necessary for the table; nor must they expect success in every crop planted. Most land must be built up. Soil is created by intelligent agricultural practices. Soil fertility, weather conditions, and many other factors enter into the success or the failure of a given crop. For an all-round homestead project the same author makes many practical suggestions based on his own experience.

Regardless of aptitudes and interests and soil fertility, by all means there should be a small piece of land where a beginning can be made in a modest way.

7. *How Much Land?*—A half acre will provide room for a home and a good garden. An acre will furnish ample room for a home, a garden, and for animal husbandry carried on on a small scale. Two or three acres perhaps would be more desirable if pasture land is desired. The cost of the land, its location, and the interest of the family in various country pursuits are all factors that should enter into the question of the size of property to be secured. For a vegetarian family, says one authority, one acre is sufficient to provide the necessary food.

8. *Cleared Land.*—Unless wood is desired for heating and cooking, there will be an advantage in securing land already cleared. Cutting trees and disposing of stumps calls for a good deal of time and work. Purchasing land that is heavily wooded will retard the agricultural program; on the other hand, if there is a sawmill near by, timber may well furnish lumber for a home, a barn, or other outbuildings at a price much below that charged at the lumberyard.

9. *Conveniences.*—The ultimate goal should embody the securing of such conveniences as contribute to the comfort and

satisfaction of living. Running water, a central heating plant in colder regions, and a bathroom should by no means be omitted. The overall plan should provide for most of the conveniences and comforts that will be found in the city home.

Gardening and Other Activities

It would seem almost axiomatic that country living should include some form of agricultural activity, at least on a part-time basis. The Spirit of Prophecy makes clear the importance of agriculture. There are great benefits to be derived from working with the soil. Regardless of the extent to which the family may wish to engage in gardening, no country living would be complete without the raising of some flowers, vegetables, and small fruits. Foods of the best quality and flavor can thus be secured, and agriculture might well form an important part of the family income, both in money saved in the family food budget and in the sale of farm products. This is why it has been urged that in the selection of home sites, good soil, or land that can be developed into good soil, should be chosen. To make a careful choice in this matter will lessen the work and disappointment and hasten the yields of valuable crops.

The Home Garden

Concerning the importance of the family garden and its potential return, both in good food and in money saved and earned, Dr. Floyd Bralliar writes:

"One of the first and most urgent problems that faces a family moving from the city into the country is the growing of a good garden. Every family should use vegetables freely in their diet every day, and the only practical way they can get these vegetables is to grow them. This is a good thing, for vegetables prepared and eaten within three or four hours of the time they are picked not only taste better but are decidedly more nutritious than vegetables bought in the store. It has been proved that most vegetables begin to lose their vitamin content within an hour after they are picked, and to a lesser degree, they gradually lose their digestibility as well.

"The inexperienced gardener usually does not realize how much food can be grown on a given area; nor does he know how to go about raising a first-class garden. The ordinary family of four should be able to grow all the vegetables they need for the year, with the exception of potatoes and corn for canning, on a plot forty by sixty feet. Many families grow all the vegetables they need on a smaller area than this, but in order to do so, they must put their ground into first-class condition and keep it thoroughly cultivated. We have received reports from many families, proving these figures to be true.

"We advise every Seventh-day Adventist who can possibly do so to grow a garden in his own backyard or on a nearby vacant lot that he can secure for this purpose. He should not expect to get rich doing this, but with careful study and painstaking work he can learn how to grow a good garden when he moves into the country. By doing this for a year or two, he will know just how to proceed when he must grow his own food.

"In order to grow a garden successfully, one must locate it where it gets at least five or six hours of sunshine every clear day, and for best results it should not be shaded at all.

"The garden plot should have good drainage. Any location where water stands for several days at any time is not naturally drained enough to grow a good garden.

"For good results, the garden must be at least forty or fifty feet from any large trees or hedge fences, for the roots of trees extend out surprisingly far, and they are likely to rob the land of its fertility and water.

"A garden can be grown on any soil, whether clay, sand, or loam; but whatever the soil is naturally, it must be enriched with humus (well-decayed vegetable matter of some kind). Before the soil is in fit condition to grow a good crop of vegetables, it must be made fertile and loose enough to admit readily both air and water, and to hold both during dry weather."

As we come to sense that we are laborers together with God, as we prepare the soil and plant the seed and cultivate the crops (see *Testimonies,* vol. 6, pp. 186, 187), the garden may become to us and our families a school in which many valuable lessons are learned. It is a means of recreation in the sense of a change of activity and physical development, and may be a worthwhile financial asset as better food products are furnished to the table at little cost from the standpoint of expenditures of money. As a spare-time hobby and recreation, gardening will yield in proportion to that which is put into it. It will call for faithful and regular attention, but it renders a satisfaction that is beyond measure.

If the expectations are not too high at the outset and the task is approached from the standpoint of an eagerness to learn, each year will show definite progress and increased returns. Emphasis should be placed on the fact that there will be some failures. If the family establishes as a goal for the first year 60 percent success and 40 percent failure, they will not be faced with the disappointment that would result from an expectation of a hundred percent success, and they may enjoy some pleasant surprises.

The interests of the family, the location of the land, and the qualities of the soil will determine the crops that can most profitably be raised. It is not our purpose here to enter into a discussion as to how to make the garden or what crops to grow. Ample counsel has been given by those who have pioneered the way.

In the development of the soil the fertilizers that come from the home dairy and the poultry are of great value and highly essential. As more and more study is given to soil fertility and the producing of food products that are not deficient in vitamins and minerals, it will be learned that there are many advantages to an all-round farm program that makes organic gardening a practical, workable arrangement. When we speak of organic gardening, we refer to the utilization of those methods and practices that restore to the earth through natural methods the elements essential to the production of the best crops. These take into account the great value of the manures produced on the place, of composting vegetable matter such as grass, leaves, and vegetable and fruit peelings, and returning those elements to the earth in a form available for immediate plant use. Some chemical fertilizers, such as 5-10-5, may be needed to augment manure and compost available. Tests of the soil will determine this.

Implements and Machinery

Limited finances may make it impossible for a newcomer to the rural community to have the needed machinery for economical work in his garden or small farm. But here again a wholesome cooperation of neighbors may make possible the exchange of the more expensive machinery such as tractor, plow, and work animals for the larger place. The new homemaker should, however, as rapidly as possible, seek to become self-contained and independent. For the family garden described above, a Rototiller of some type is almost indispensable. This can be secured for a few hundred dollars, and if well cared for will serve for many years.

Milk, Eggs, and Honey

For the family there are many advantages and economies in having a home dairy. A steady supply of milk and butterfat, with but small expenditure for feeds purchased, is a large factor in "have-more" living. The preferences of the family, the size and location of the property, and the disposal of surplus milk are all factors to be taken into account in the choice of a cow or goats.

Whereas a cow should have about two acres of pasture, two milk goats will do well on one acre. One goat requires only one sixth the amount of feed required by a cow. If goats are kept, it is well to have two. They can be cared for in half the time called for by a cow, and each will furnish from two to six quarts of milk a day. With two, the supply can extend throughout the year.

A few hives of bees will produce a large part of the sweets needed by the family with very little time and small space devoted to their care. A few chickens will supply eggs for kitchen use.

Life at Its Best

"The great Master Himself blessed the work of tilling the soil."—*Country Living,* p. 14.

"A secluded home in the Galilean hills; a household sustained by honest, self-respecting labor; a life of simplicity; daily conflict with difficulty and hardship; self-sacrifice, economy, and patient, gladsome service; the hour of study at His mother's side, with the open scroll of Scripture; the quiet of dawn or twilight in the green valley; the holy ministries of nature; the study of creation and providence; and the soul's communion with God—these were the conditions and opportunities of the early life of Jesus."—*Ibid.,* p. 15.

For a family to move from the city to a home on the land is probably one of the most vitally important events in a lifetime. It calls for serious thought and should be approached with prayer and consultation on the part of every member of the family. And yet, as one author wrote: "To give up city life and move to the country is a perfectly attainable dream."

The Pioneer Spirit

The step contemplated corresponds, on the family level, to the coming to America of our forefathers. They left their European homes in search of freedom of thought and worship, education for their children, and a security they were forbidden in the Old World. Their hardships as they carved a home in the New England wilderness is a familiar story. Their supplies were the most meager, their homes were the simplest. Their food was produced from virgin soil snatched from the forests. They ate what they could raise, they spun the yarn and wove the cloth for their garments.

A similar spirit of bravery and endurance marked the following generations who pioneered the far stretches of the continent. Each section of our country, as it has been opened up, has been occupied by those who were activated by the spirit of daring, of ability to endure hardships for the future benefits of which they dreamed.

Every religious movement has been characterized by the same spirit on the part of its promoters. The founders of the Seventh-day Adventist denomination had a similar experience. The same stalwart, self-denying spirit is needed in a degree by families who choose to move to the country. Let the determination be right, and good results will follow.

Security and Insecurity

Fear of the future shadows the rising generation. It dogs the steps of old and young. There is fear of war, fear of loss of position and earning capacity, fear of competition, fear on all sides that is depressing the minds of many. With the picture given by statesmen, scientists, leaders in business, and the Scriptures as well, this feeling of fear is not groundless.

Christians with faith in the Word of God will greatly increase their security by moving from the city to a home on the land. The insecurity of city positions and employment will increase, oppressive times are before us, and if for no other reason than for added security, our lay church members should find their place in the country. "I see the necessity of the people of God moving out of the cities into retired country [places] where they may cultivate the land and raise their own produce. . . . I see the necessity of making haste to get all things ready for the crisis."—*Country Living,* p. 21. But go not to the country for temporal security alone. Seek your place on the land for the fuller, richer life you will find there.

Make a home worthy of the name, not merely a shelter from heat and storm or from the atomic bomb. Make it a place of peace and contentment, of progressive development of the intellectual and spiritual nature. Make it a school for the children and parents, a medical center for the community where all will learn of the broader, fuller joy of right living.

The surroundings of the country home, the house itself, the

grounds, the woods, the shop, the growing things—all are part of the educational program, not to mention the pictures that illustrate the texts they study as they plan the season's garden or the poultry houses or the new barn. The list is endless, for in such surroundings there is limitless opportunity for advancement for both parents and children in this school of living.

These are a few of the acquisitions of independence that come with the acquiring of a country home and its development by a progressive family. They are more than can be enumerated and will be appreciated in proportion as the country living reaches its full development. The move to the country should be a veritable emancipation. In addition to the freedoms enjoyed by the man of the world who moves out, the Seventh-day Adventist family should come to an enjoyment as much in advance of his as their faith and hope is in advance of his. You will begin to understand why the Saviour loved to go early to the woods and hillsides for communion with His Father, and why in His teaching He often drew His lessons from nature.

We would suggest that after you are fully settled in a new rural home, you list the gains you have made in the realm of independence and behold how astonishingly long that list becomes.

The Lure of the Land

Selections From the Writings of Ellen G. White

No Improvement of God's Plan

"In God's plan for Israel, every family had a home on the land, with sufficient ground for tilling. Thus were provided both the means and the incentive for a useful, industrious, and self-supporting life. And no devising of men has ever improved upon that plan. To the world's departure from it is owing, to a large degree, the poverty and wretchedness that exist today."—*Counsels to Parents and Teachers,* pp. 275, 276.

The Care of Plants and Animals

"By the distribution of the land among the people, God provided for them, as for the dwellers in Eden, the occupation most favorable to development—the care of plants and animals."—*Education,* p. 43.

Tillers of the Soil

"The men who held fast God's principles of life dwelt among the fields and hills. They were tillers of the soil, and keepers of flocks and herds; and in this free, independent life, with its opportunities for labor and study and meditation, they learned of God, and taught their children of His works and ways."—*Ibid.,* pp. 33, 34.

ABC of Education

"Working the soil is one of the best kinds of employment, calling the muscles into action and resting the mind. Study in agricultural lines should be the A, B, and C of the education given in our schools. This is the very first work that should be entered upon. . . . Our youth need an education in felling trees and tilling the soil as well as in literary lines."—*Testimonies,* vol. 6, p. 179.

Agriculture in the School

"No line of manual training is of more value than agriculture. A greater effort should be made to create and to encourage an interest in agricultural pursuits. Let the teacher call attention to what the Bible says about agriculture: that it was God's plan for man to till the earth; that the first man, the ruler of the whole world, was given a garden to cultivate; and that many of the world's greatest men, its real nobility, have been tillers of the soil. Show the opportunities in such a life. The wise man says, 'The king himself is served by the field.' Of him who cultivates the soil the Bible declares, 'His God doth instruct him to discretion, and doth teach him.' And again, 'Whoso keepeth the fig-tree shall eat the fruit thereof.' He who earns his livelihood by agriculture escapes many temptations and enjoys unnumbered privileges and blessings denied to those whose work lies in the great cities. And in these days of mammoth trusts and business competition, there are few who enjoy so real an independence and so great certainty of fair return for their labor as does the tiller of the soil.

"In the study of agriculture, let pupils be given not only theory, but practice. While they learn what science can teach in regard to the nature and preparation of the soil, the value of different crops, and the best methods of production, let them put their knowledge to use. Let teachers share the work with the students, and show what results can be achieved through skilful, intelligent effort. Thus may be awakened a genuine interest, an ambition to do the work in the best possible manner. Such an ambition, together with the invigorating effect of exercise, sunshine, and pure air, will create a love for agricultural labor that with many youth will determine their choice of an occupation. Thus might be set on foot influences that would go far in turning the tide of migration which now sets so strongly toward the great cities.

"Thus also our schools could aid effectively in the disposition of the unemployed masses. Thousands of helpless and starving beings, whose numbers are daily swelling the ranks of the criminal classes, might achieve self-support in a happy, healthy, independent life if they could be directed in skilful, diligent labor in the tilling of the soil."—*Education,* pp. 219, 220.

Lessons From Agricultural Procedures

"It would be well if there were, connected with every school, lands for cultivation. Such lands should be regarded as God's own schoolroom. The things of nature should be looked upon as a lesson book which His children are to study, and from which they may obtain knowledge as to the culture of the soil.

"In tilling the soil, in disciplining and subduing the land, lessons may constantly be learned. No one would think of settling upon a raw piece of land, expecting it at once to yield a harvest. Earnestness, diligence, and persevering labor are to be put forth in treating the soil preparatory to sowing the seed. So it is in the spiritual work in the human heart. Those who would be benefited by the tilling of the soil must go forth with the word of God in their hearts. They will then find the fallow ground of the heart broken by the softening, subduing influence of the Holy Spirit. Unless hard work is bestowed on the soil, it will not yield a harvest. So with the soil of the heart: the Spirit of God must work upon it, to refine and discipline it, before it can bring forth fruit to the glory of God.

"The soil will not produce its riches when worked by impulse. It needs thoughtful, daily attention. It must be plowed often and deep, with a view to keeping out the weeds that take nourishment from the good seed planted. Thus those who plow and sow prepare for the harvest. None need stand in the field amid the sad wreck of their hopes.

"The blessing of the Lord will rest upon those who thus work the land, learning spiritual lessons from nature. In cultivating the soil the worker knows little what treasures will open up before him. While he is not to despise the instruction he may gather from minds that have had an experience and from the information that intelligent men may impart, he should gather lessons for himself. This is a part of his training. The cultivation of the soil will prove an education to the soul."—*Christ's Object Lessons,* pp. 87, 88.

Soil Improvement—Develop Capacity of the Soil

"'The working of the land will be a special blessing to the worker. There is a great want of intelligent men to till the soil, who will be thorough. This knowledge will not be a hindrance to the education essential for business or for usefulness in any line. To develop the capacity of the soil requires thought and intelligence. Not only will it develop muscle, but capability for study, because the action of brain and muscle is equalized. We should so train the youth that they will love to work upon the land, and delight in improving it. . . .

"'He who taught Adam and Eve in Eden how to tend the garden, would instruct men today. There is wisdom for him who holds the plow, and plants and sows the seed. The earth has its concealed treasures, and the Lord would have thousands and tens of thousands working upon the soil who are crowded into the cities to watch for a chance to earn a trifle.'"—*Life Sketches,* pp. 354, 355.

God's Plan for Restoring Land Fertility

"Through disobedience to God, Adam and Eve had lost Eden, and because of sin the whole earth was cursed. But if God's people followed His instruction, their land would be restored to fertility and beauty. God Himself gave them directions in regard to the culture of the soil, and they were to cooperate with Him in its restoration."—*Christ's Object Lessons,* p. 289.

"There is much mourning over unproductive soil, when if men would read the Old Testament Scriptures they would see that the Lord knew much better than they in regard to the proper treatment of land. After being cultivated for several years, and giving her treasure to the possession of man, portions of the land should be allowed to rest, and then the crops should be changed."—*Fundamentals of Christian Education,* p. 323.

E. G. White—A Pioneer Agriculturist

"We passed through many interesting experiences while in Australia.* We helped establish a school from the foundation, going into the eucalyptus woods and camping while the trees were being felled, the grounds cleared, and the school building erected. . . .

"We did what we could to develop our land, and encouraged

* 1891-1900.

our neighbors to cultivate the soil, that they, too, might have fruit and vegetables of their own. We taught them how to prepare the soil, and what to plant, and how to take care of the growing produce. They soon learned the advantages of providing for themselves in this way."—Manuscript 126, 1902.

Recounting Avondale's Objectives

"I came here [Avondale] and began work on my place so earnestly that it inspired all with fresh zeal, and they have been working with a will, rejoicing that they have the privilege. We have provoked one another to zeal and good works. The school workers were afraid I would plant the first trees, and now both they and I have the satisfaction of having the first genuine orchards in this vicinity. Some of our trees will yield fruit next year, and the peaches will bear quite a crop in two years. . . .

"The school has made an excellent beginning. The students are learning how to plant trees, strawberries, et cetera; how they must keep every sprangle and fiber of the roots uncramped in order to give them a chance to grow. . . . Men and women and children are wanted who will work the land, and use their tact and skill, not with a feeling that they are menials, but that they are doing just such noble work as God gave to Adam and Eve in Eden, who loved to see the miracles wrought by the divine Husbandman. The human agent plants the seed, and God waters it, and causes His sun to shine upon it, and up springs the tiny blade. . . .

"We should work the soil cheerfully, hopefully, gratefully, believing that the earth holds in her bosom rich stores for the faithful worker to garner, richer than gold or silver. The niggardliness laid to her charge is false witness. With proper, intelligent cultivation, the earth will yield its treasures for the benefit of man. . . .

"The cultivation of our land requires the exercise of all the brain power and tact we possess. The lands around us testify to the indolence of men. We hope to arouse to action the dormant senses. We hope to see intelligent farmers, who will be rewarded for their earnest labor. The hand and heart must cooperate, bringing new and sensible plans into operation in the cultivation of the soil. We have here seen the giant trees felled and uprooted, we have seen the plowshare pressed into the earth, turning deep furrows for the planting of young trees, and the sowing of the seed. The students are learning what plowing means, and that the hoe and shovel, the rake and the harrow, are all implements of honorable and profitable industry. Mistakes will often be made, but error lies close beside truth. Wisdom will be learned by failures, and the energy that will make a beginning gives hope of success in the end. Hesitation will keep things back, precipitancy will alike retard, but all will serve as lessons if the human agents will have it so.

"In the school that is started here in Cooranbong, we look to see real success in agricultural lines, combined with a study of the sciences. We mean for this place to be a center, from which shall irradiate light, precious advanced knowledge that shall result in the working of unimproved lands, so that hills and valleys shall blossom like the rose. For both children and men, labor combined with mental taxation will give the right kind of all-round education. The cultivation of the mind will bring tact and fresh incentives to the cultivation of the soil.

"There will be a new presentation of men as breadwinners, possessing educated, trained ability to work the soil to advantage. Their minds will not be overtaxed and strained to the uttermost with the study of the sciences. Such men will break down the foolish sentiments that have prevailed in regard to manual labor. An influence will go forth, not in loud-voiced oratory, but in real inculcation of ideas. We shall see farmers who are not coarse and rough and slack, careless of their apparel and of the appearance of their homes; but they will bring taste into farmhouses. Rooms will be sunny and inviting. We shall not see blackened ceilings, covered with cloth full of dust and dirt. Science, genius, intelligence, will be manifest in the home. The cultivation of the soil will be regarded as elevating and ennobling. Pure, practical religion will be manifested in treating the earth as God's treasure house. The more intelligent a man becomes, the more should religious influence be radiating from him. And the Lord would have us treat the earth as a precious treasure, lent us in trust."—*Testimonies to Ministers,* pp. 242-245.

Avondale as Ellen White Saw It

"I have planned what can be raised in different places. I have said, 'Here can be a crop of alfalfa, there can be strawberries, here can be sweet corn and common corn, and this ground will raise good potatoes, while that will raise good fruit of all kinds.' So in imagination I have all the different places in a flourishing condition. No one need to regret in reference to this land, for with proper working it will surprise the people in this section of the country."—Letter 14, 1894.

A Work for Christian Farmers

"Christian farmers can do real missionary work in helping the poor to find homes on the land, and in teaching them how to till the soil and make it productive. Teach them how to use the implements of agriculture, how to cultivate various crops, how to plant and care for orchards.

"Many who till the soil fail to secure adequate returns because of their neglect. Their orchards are not properly cared for, the crops are not put in at the right time, and a mere surface work is done in cultivating the soil. Their ill success they charge to the unproductiveness of the land. False witness is often borne in condemning land that, if properly worked, would yield rich returns. The narrow plans, the little strength put forth, the little study as to the best methods, call loudly for reform.

"Let proper methods be taught to all who are willing to learn. If any do not wish you to speak to them of advanced ideas, let the lessons be given silently. Keep up the culture of your own land. Drop a word to your neighbors when you can, and let the harvest be eloquent in favor of right methods. Demonstrate what can be done with the land when properly worked."—*The Ministry of Healing,* p. 193.

With God's Blessing

"God can bless twenty acres of land, and make them as productive as one hundred."—*Testimonies,* vol. 5, p. 152.

Ellen G. White Instructed in Planting Fruit Trees

"While we were in Australia, we adopted the . . . plan . . . of digging deep trenches and filling them in with dressing that would create good soil. This we did in the cultivation of tomatoes, oranges, lemons, peaches, and grapes.

"The man of whom we purchased our peach trees told me that he would be pleased to have me observe the way they were planted. I then asked him to let me show him how it had been represented in the night season that they should be planted. I ordered my hired man to dig a deep cavity in the ground, then put in rich dirt, then stones, then rich dirt. After this he put in layers of earth and dressing until the hole was filled. I told the nurseryman that I had planted in this way in the rocky soil in America. I invited him to visit me when these fruits should be ripe. He said to me, 'You need no lesson from me to teach you how to plant the trees.'

"Our crops were very successful. The peaches were the most beautiful in coloring, and the most delicious in flavor of any that I had tasted. We grew the large yellow Crawford and other varieties, grapes, apricots, nectarines, and plums."—Letter 350, 1907; *Selected Messages,* book 3, p. 328.

The Spraying of Fruit Trees

"There are those who say that nothing, not even insects, should be killed. God has not entrusted any such message to His people. It is possible to stretch the command 'Thou shalt not kill' to any limit; but it is not according to sound reasoning to do this. Those who do it have not learned in the school of Christ.

"This earth has been cursed because of sin, and in these last days vermin of every kind will multiply. These pests must be killed, or they will annoy and torment and even kill us, and destroy the work of our hands and the fruit of our land. In places there are ants [termites] which entirely destroy the woodwork of houses. Should not these be destroyed? Fruit trees must be sprayed, that the insects which would spoil the fruit may be killed. God has given us a part to act, and this part we must act with faithfulness. Then we can leave the rest with the Lord.

"God has given no man the message, Kill not ant or flea or moth. Troublesome and harmful insects and reptiles we must guard against and destroy, to preserve ourselves and our possessions from harm. And even if we do our best to exterminate these pests, they will still multiply."—Manuscript 70, 1901; *Selected Messages,* book 3, p. 329.

Enterprises Operated for the Lord Versus Worldly Enterprises

Defining the Terms

"Not one in a hundred among us is doing anything beyond engaging in common, worldly enterprises."—*Testimonies,* vol. 8, p. 148.

"We have no time now to give our energies and talents to worldly enterprises. Shall we become absorbed in serving the world, serving ourselves, and lose eternal life?"—*Ibid.,* vol. 9, p. 104.

Two objectives in all we do—two distinct types of businesses, or enterprises—are pointed out by the pen of inspiration. God's people are warned against engaging in worldly enterprises, and on the other hand they are directed to devote their energies, time, and talents to enterprises that contribute to the advancement of His work in the world.

Whether an occupation or enterprise is to be classified as worldly or for God depends very largely upon the attitude or motive of the operator. Enterprises conducted for personal gain engage a large part of the energies of the members of our churches today. The Lord has a right to expect the consecration of the time, talents, and abilities of every church member, but He tells us that ninety-nine out of every one hundred are forgetful of their debt to Him and are working for themselves.

This explains why the Lord's enterprises are neglected. The first chapter of Haggai tells why the work of the Lord in the world advances so slowly, and why the end has not come long before this. By our dilatory habits in following the counsel in matters of occupation we are hindering the cause of the Lord.

As city dwellers seeking a home on the land, let us find our place in the field, the business, or the enterprise, and fill it to the glory of God, as did Joseph in his experience in Egypt.

Agriculture Should Be a Leading Enterprise for the Lord

"If the poor now crowded into the cities could find homes upon the land, they might not only earn a livelihood, but find health and happiness now unknown to them. . . . Many would learn the lesson of dependence upon Him. Through nature they would hear His voice speaking to their hearts of His peace and love, and mind and soul and body would respond to the healing, life-giving power."—*The Ministry of Healing,* pp. 190-192.

The soil, a living thing, responds to proper handling. To produce results, it must be worked "cheerfully, hopefully, gratefully" for "the earth holds in her bosom rich stores for the faithful worker to garner, stores richer than gold or silver."—*Testimonies,* vol. 6, p. 178.

The Christian farmer and his children, to get the full results of their labor with the soil, need to remember that they are working hand in hand with the Creator of the worlds. With this mental attitude their work will be a joy, their hearts will be filled with praise, and the neighbors will find in them a new type of farmer.

Missionary Work for Farmers

"Christian farmers can do real missionary work in helping the poor to find homes on the land, and in teaching them how to till the soil and make it productive."—*The Ministry of Healing,* p. 193.

"There are multitudes of poor families for whom no better missionary work could be done than to assist them in settling on the land and in learning how to make it yield them a livelihood."—*Ibid.,* p. 192.

"He who taught Adam and Eve in Eden how to tend the garden, desires to instruct men today. There is wisdom for him who drives the plow and sows the seed. . . . Let them move forward courageously, trusting in Him to supply their needs according to the riches of His goodness. . . . Look heavenward in faith."—*Ibid.,* p. 200.

Mechanical Enterprises Operated for the Lord

"Missionary families are needed to settle in the waste places. Let farmers, financiers, builders, and those who are skilled in various arts and crafts, go to neglected fields, to improve the land, to establish industries, to prepare humble homes for themselves, and to help their neighbors. . . . This is the work we are called to do."—*Ibid.,* p. 194.

The farmer would be greatly handicapped were it not for the assistance of a skilled machinist. The blacksmith shop by the side of the road—or the auto-repair shop in these modern days—calls for a skilled craftsman, and one whose heart is afire with love for the Creator will prove a blessing to his community.

William Carey, missionary in India, cobbled shoes to earn his livelihood, but his real business was to preach the gospel. The shoe-repair shop is needed in the rural community today.

The apostle Paul made tents in the shop of Aquila and Priscilla in order to support himself and his colaborers. But his real business in life was to reach the hearts and souls of men, and the tentmaker's shop brought him in contact with people he could not meet in any other way.

The mechanic, the dressmaker, the appliance repairman, and the dry cleaner are in demand, and godly men and women have here an avenue to the hearts of weary, soul-sick humanity.

Jesus Christ spent the greater part of His sojourn on earth in the carpenter shop in Nazareth. He was well known to the builders of His community for the high-class work He turned out as a cabinetmaker. Home building and furniture making is one of the real problems in every move from city to rural site. The Christian mechanic may be a torch bearer for the Master.

Every trade, every handicraft, that has a converted mind behind it can find a place in the Lord's plan by which the possessor can earn his living and at the same time minister to the needs of humanity in His name.

Learn to Be Self-sustaining

A Glimpse of History

The United States, established in the providence of God, has been a refuge for millions fleeing from the oppression of countries across the seas. They came here in search of religious rights; they sought the right to educate their children in the principles of Protestantism and the faith of their fathers. They came because here the common man had the right to carry on his business and pursuits without the unreasonable interference of government and to earn a livelihood far beyond that possible in some other lands.

The lamblike character of this government invited their confidence and rewarded their industry. Wide areas here have been made productive by the labor of these immigrants, and their generations have contributed to the wealth of this country. But for a number of years the gentle voice of democracy has been growing harsh and still harsher. Men and women now living have felt the sting of laws that controlled the crops they raised, the prices of their products, the amounts they could sell. They have learned the meaning of that Scripture statement that men will be forbidden to buy or sell.

Labor Organizations

Organizations of the laboring men and women in mines and factories, in transportation on land and sea, originated to protect the rights of the laborer, have exerted pressure on the legislative and executive branches of the government until at times they are able, under provocation, to hold up traffic, to disrupt city industries and utilities, even to the point where life is endangered. Not uncommon are strikes that have interfered with the distribution of milk for infants and other necessary food products.

Such events are but a foretaste of impending laws. The gentle voice of the original government of the land in time becomes the roar of the dragon. And that time is fast approaching. (See *Country Living,* pp. 9-12.)

Rural Industries and the Land a Means of Support

Forewarning of these times and conditions, God has bidden His people to move from the cities and secure homes on the land. We are told not to build our institutions in the cities, but to locate sanitariums, publishing houses, schools, and food-manufacturing plants in the country. In 1905, Ellen White wrote:

"Light has been given that the large cities are to become as Sodom and Gomorrah. . . . Parents should now do everything in their power to redeem their neglect, and place their children where they will be under the very best influences. . . .

"God has sent warning after warning that our schools and publishing houses and sanitariums are to be established out of the city, in places where the youth may be taught most effectively what is truth. Let no one attempt to use the *Testimonies* to vindicate the establishment of large business interests in the cities. . . .

"The cities will become worse and worse. In them will be strife and bloodshed, and at last they will be visited by earthquakes. Buildings will be thrown down, and will be consumed by fire from heaven. . . .

"The cities must be worked. Those who are living in them must be warned of what is before us. Let time and means be wisely spent. See if you cannot do something in the highways and byways of the cities to proclaim the message of present truth.

"But do not locate your families in the city, and do not establish business interests there. . . . Watchers will be set to seek occasion of complaint against the commandment-keeping people of God. Satan will exercise his power and enmity, and oppression will be the result. The larger the city, the greater will be the oppression. . . .

"Though stormy times are before us, much missionary work still remains to be done in the cities. . . . But this does not require the establishment of large business enterprises."—Manuscript 76,

1905.

These warnings heeded will place the obedient on vantage ground. By carefully following nature's laws in the cultivation of the soil, families can cause the earth to yield its treasures and can produce a part or all of the food needed for their own use and a surplus for the less fortunate. By foresight and good management they can make much of their clothing, their houses, and their furniture, and be the better physically and spiritually for so doing.

Life under those conditions will be much more simple than now. Our physical needs can be provided, but we must follow on to know the Lord. We must learn how to do what He has advised us as a people to do.

Legislative enactments restricting liberty will first be felt in the cities. Those living on the land will be longest free from laws compelling government control, regimentation of industry, exorbitant taxation, and restricting freedom of speech and of worship.

A Word of Caution

While Ellen White wrote of the farm as the sole support for families—and it can be so under favorable circumstances—the developments of the past two or three decades, with mechanized crop production and increased costs of farm equipment and everything that must be purchased, together with tuition costs in educating the children, the family farm is losing much of its lure and the promise of independence and comfortable support.

This pamphlet is aimed at encouraging and giving guidance to the city family who is turning to the country. To such—not too well-versed in the science of commercial crop production—it may be well to restrict the pursuit of agricultural activities more to the family garden. This can be very productive and rewarding, yielding bountifully for the family, and perhaps even some to be shared with neighbors. But the facts in the case would indicate that families would do well to locate in situations where there is a cash income from family-owned-and-operated industries, shops, or full-time employment in a wage-earning activity.

Farming is rewarding, but it seems that under present conditions in the United States, it is for the experienced and skilled, backed with a reasonable financial base. Gardening, however, has its multiple benefits to the family and should not by any means be neglected in the country living setting.

An Impressive Example From History

The command to leave the city and to prepare to meet labor union problems and oppressive legislation has been sounded for many decades. Our day is compared to the history of the Jews as they approached the fall of their kingdom and the overthrow of Jerusalem by the Roman Empire. They had a last long call to flee from the city before armed forces surrounded Jerusalem for the final assault. There is another parallel in the earlier history of the Jewish nation. We read:

"The decree that will finally go forth against the remnant people of God will be very similar to that issued by Ahasuerus against the Jews. Today the enemies of the true church see in the little company keeping the Sabbath commandment, a Mordecai at the gate. The reverence of God's people for His law is a constant rebuke to those who have cast off the fear of the Lord and are trampling on His Sabbath."—*Prophets and Kings,* p. 605.

Make Haste

The Scripture calls attention to the experience of Lot and his wife, who lingered too long in the city of Sodom. "Had Lot hastened as the Lord desired him to, his wife would not have become a pillar of salt. Lot had too much of a lingering spirit. Let us not be like him."—*Country Living,* p. 6.

"Satan knows that his time is short. As we draw near to the close of time, the cities will become more and more corrupt, and more and more objectionable as places for establishing centers of our work. The dangers of travel will increase, confusion and drunkenness will abound; and if there can be found places in retired mountain regions, where it would be difficult for the evils of the cities to enter, let our people secure such places for our sanitariums and advanced schools. . . .

"Who will be warned? We say again, Out of the cities. Do not consider it a great deprivation, that you must go into the hills and mountains, but seek for that retirement where you can be alone with God, to learn His will and way. . . . Do not consider it a privation when you are called to leave the cities and move out into country places. Here there await rich blessings for those who will grasp them. By beholding the scenes of nature, the works of the Creator, by studying God's handiwork, imperceptibly you will be changed into the same image."—Manuscript 85, 1908.

It is most important that in this very hour our people find their place on the land, and learn there to feed, clothe, and shelter their families. In this little time of peace (and how short it will be, no man knows), the wise will obey the command "Get out of the cities."

Vital Role of Church Leadership

"Let there be wise generalship in this matter, and all move under the guidance of a wise, unseen Counselor, which is God." "Some men have insight into matters, having ability to counsel. It is a gift of God."—*Country Living,* pp. 26, 27.

So important is the move of a family from the city to a new home on the land that the Lord has given instruction on various phases of such a project, and He has given wisdom to men of experience to guide and counsel. The Lord has added specific instruction as to the caution with which such a marked change in life should be made. Those who find themselves in this situation can do no better than to read carefully such paragraphs as the following quoted from the Spirit of Prophecy.

Study Carefully. Be Levelheaded.—"Let there be nothing done in a disorderly manner, that there shall be a great loss or sacrifice made upon property because of ardent, impulsive speeches which stir up an enthusiasm which is not after the order of God, that a victory that was essential to be gained, shall, for lack of levelheaded moderation and proper contemplation and sound principles and purposes, be turned into a defeat."—*Ibid.,* p. 27.

Take Time to Pray. Seek Wise Counsel.—"Let all be careful what they say; if they know not the mind of God in some matters, let them never speak from a guess or suppose so. If they know nothing definite, let them say so, and let the individual rely wholly upon God. Let there be much praying done, and even with fasting."—*Ibid.*

Some Men May Counsel; Some May Not.—"Some men have insight into matters, having ability to counsel. It is a gift of God. In moments when the cause of God is in need of words, sound and solemn and solid, they can speak words which will lead minds perplexed and in darkness, to see as a quick flash of sunlight the course for them to pursue. . . . There is an unraveling, a clearing up of the path before them, and the Lord has let His sunlight in, and they see their prayers are answered. . . .

"While some teachers may be strong and efficient in teaching in the lines of Bible doctrines, they will not all be men who have a knowledge of practical life, and can advise perplexed minds with surety and safety. They do not discern the perplexing situation that must necessarily come to every family who shall make a change."—*Ibid.*, pp. 26, 27.

A Final Word

It is wise to keep in touch with the presidents of your local conferences over the problem of location, for they are men of experience, and they are vitally interested. Your pastor also should be consulted.

It is well, as far as possible, to have families settle in their own State or community rather than to move any great distance. Church members of one section should be able to do their best work in their own locality, generally speaking, and should be interested in contributing their efforts to building the church work in their own neighborhood.

One of the important matters many church members face today is the locating of their families in the country and doing it in such a way that it will redound to the glory of God. In the first place, such a move calls for a change of mind and manner of living. It cannot be accomplished without a true conversion and considerable dedication to God's plan of living for His people. God has rich blessings in store for those who are guided in their lives by His counsels to His people.

Before closing this pamphlet, please read the 1978 Annual Council action on country living that follows.

Appendix

VOTED, To adopt the following document on country living:

1. *Institutional Development and Relocation*

a. That in the planning and development of new building programs for medical institutions, publishing houses, offices, colleges and boarding academies, the following counsel be taken into consideration:

1) That such institutions be located outside of heavily populated urban areas, but within reasonable access to such areas.

2) That such institutions be located where workers may follow the counsel, " 'We must make wise plans to warn the cities, and at the same time live where we can shield our children and ourselves from the contaminating and demoralizing influences so prevalent in these places.' "—*Life Sketches,* p. 410.

3) That plans for new institutions be as modest and economical as possible.

b. That boards of large institutions whose surroundings have changed to an urban environment and who are facing major rebuilding programs be sensitive to the counsels regarding the locations of these institutions as stated by Ellen G. White as to the ideal locations for such institutions.

2. *Evangelistic Outreach*

a. That we give priority in our evangelistic planning to the massive challenge of the large cities, and that we plan for our work in these cities in harmony with the inspired counsels of Ellen G. White.

1) "The cities are to be worked from the outposts. Said the messenger of God, 'Shall not the cities be warned? Yes, not by God's people living in them, but by their visiting them, to warn

them of what is coming upon the earth.' "—*Evangelism,* p. 77.

2) "All that Lot and his family did in Sodom could have been done by them, even if they had lived in a place some distance away from the city. Enoch walked with God, and yet he did not live in the midst of any city polluted with every kind of violence and wickedness, as did Lot in Sodom."—*Ibid.,* p. 78.

3) "It is God's design that our people should locate outside the cities, and from these outposts warn the cities."—*Ibid.,* p. 76.

3. *Counsels to Church Members*

a. That church members be urged to study the counsels to move out of the large and heavily populated cities to areas that are more rural or to smaller towns, keeping in mind the following principles:

1) That city to country living does not necessarily mean city to farm situations miles removed from city areas, but it means relocation to more rural or small-town areas conducive to the spiritual and physical welfare of the family, where land for a garden is available.

2) That country living does not necessitate purchasing a farm but might entail the operation of a small business or industry.

3) That a good piece of land where a good water supply and garden space are available would be desirable.

4) That individuals should find employment or seek self-employment sufficient to sustain their families before moving from the cities to rural areas, thus avoiding discouragement and a subsequent move back to the city.

5) That some members could well move from large cities to smaller, unentered towns or counties and begin work to raise up a memorial to the Lord as self-supporting workers.

b. That arrangements be made to republish the pamphlet *From City to Country Living,* so that church members contemplating a change in home location may have opportunity to secure and study this pamphlet, along with the counsel given in the pamphlet *Country Living,* by Ellen G. White.

c. That church leaders, Spirit of Prophecy directors, or other persons appointed for this purpose in the union and local conferences make themselves acquainted with the counsels regarding these matters and seek to guide our church members who may be contemplating a move to a more rural area.

d. That while these counsels are kept before the members as ideals toward which they should prayerfully strive, it should be recognized that there are many new converts whose economic situation makes it practically impossible to immediately follow this counsel. Therefore, efforts should be made to suggest alternative measures for such persons so they can raise and train their families as nearly as possible in harmony with the guidelines for country living.